£2-

Hannah Raymond-Cox grew up in Hong Kong and San Francisco, and has bounced around the UK since age sixteen. She studied International Relations and Modern History at St Andrews alongside her career in poetry and her work includes original plays, slam poetry pieces, and bespoke poems. Hannah won the Stanza Slam, was a National Poetry Slam Championships Finalist for Scotland, and performed on the BBC Stage at the Edinburgh Fringe. She has gigged everywhere from the Royal Albert Hall to a tiny dive bar in Hong Kong. When she is stressed she makes meringues.

GW00514652

Amuse Girl

Hannah Raymond-Cox

Burning Eye

BurningEyeBooks
Never Knowingly
Mainstream

This edition published by Burning Eye Books 2019

www.burningeye.co.uk

@burningeyebooks

Burning Eye Books

15 West Hill, Portishead, BS20 6LG

ISBN 978-1-911570-60-8

Amuse Girl

APERITIF

'Amuse Girl' is a very bad pun on *amuse-gueule*, a free small dish sent out by the chef to awaken the diner's palate before a posh meal. The concept of *amuse-gueule* is also unfairly perceived as slightly naughty because *gueule* is equivalent to *gob*. It's been hypercorrected to *amuse-bouche* in English-speaking countries. This is hilarious because it's still a filthy concept if your brain wants to interrogate the translation (is *gob-amuser* so much worse than *mouth-amuser*?). Despite the renaming, the unpredictable and inherently sensual nature of the *amuse-gueule* shines through.

From an elaborate imitation of caviar that turns out to be mushroom essence to just a blob of wasabi, I've had more *amuses* than hot dinners. Which makes sense, because they're little touches of ideas. A good poem is a little touch of a big idea. The following are poems intended to enliven the palate, satiate the mind, and make you feel like you've been on a weird-ass culinary journey. Please dig in!

MENU

AMUSE-GUEULES

NEIGHBOURHOOD

A MELTING 99

SEMAPHORISM/SUNRISE BUMBLE BEE TOMATO

RADISH/RAVISH

A SLICE OF GEODUCK WITH NATTO AND SPRING ONIONS

OLIVE + CAVIAR THE WRONG WAY ROUND

RICE PAPER FLOWERS WITH RASPBERRY CENTRES

GIN MERINGUE

DINNER SERVICE

BREAD PLATE

BUTTER KNIFE

OYSTER FORK

SALAD OR FRUIT FORK

FISH FORK

MEAT FORK

SERVICE PLATE

CARVING KNIFE

MEAT KNIFE

FISH KNIFE

SALAD OR FRUIT KNIFE

SOUP SPOON

DESSERT SPOON

DESSERT FORK

TEASPOON

NAPKIN

LIBATIONS

WATER GLASS

CHAMPAGNE GLASS

WHITE WINE GLASS

RED WINE GLASS

BEER GLASS

WHISKY TUMBLER

ESPRESSO CUP

TEAPOT

COURSES

SOUP

SALAD

FISH

MAIN COURSE

PALATE CLEANSER

HARD CHEESES

SOFT CHEESES

DESSERT

AFTER DINNER MINT

A BURP

AMUSE-GUEULES

NEIGHBOURHOOD

Tasting notes: dropped crust

arthur really set up an unachievable dream and so did mr
rogers i baked a pie for my next-door neighbours and they
don't eat pie why i don't get neighbourhoods i barely know
my landlady never mind the people who live a whole closed
door away they shut that door in my mug my pie hit their
welcome mat—

A MELTING 99

Tasting notes: decaying nostalgia

england [1]
england [2]
england [3]
england [4]
england [5]
england [6]
england [7]

england   as real as george orwell/eliot/curious

---

1   cf. my jerusalem   my holy land   my home   green
            pleasant   fields   rushing of wind o'er t' moors

2   see: rattling carriages   stand and deliver cosy roadside
         public houses   ubiquity of blacksmiths chalk

3   viz. spires of stone   barristers bewigged   wool-sack
             squat crenellated buildings   grey

4   e.g. holiday camps   john susan titty roger peter susan
         edmund lucy julian dick anne george   lashings of
         ginger beer   cream buns   nice flask of grog
         red white and blue

5   no signal: jolly pleasant place

6   contra. never existed

7   see also: the worst form of historical revisionism

SEMAPHORISM/SUNRISE BUMBLE BEE TOMATO

Tasting notes: a lone salted heirloom tomato tastes how the gradual sun rising looks

hello
see me waving my flag from this
far far hill

hello?

we can sit in a ditch together
apart
on our own hill
and stare at the sky above and the valley below
and wonder how to get down

you just wave
if you need

RADISH/RAVISH

Tasting notes: it's a bit of japanese radish on a spoon

every time our eyes
meet!
i feel like
i just ate a whole blob of cheap wasabi paste
(in a good way)
or
i slid down the stone slide with my fingers only barely
holding on to the cardboard boogie board and managed to
stick the sandy landing without tumbling immediately after
my feet get under me

the tumbling is just
inside
triumphant

A SLICE OF GEODUCK WITH NATTO AND SPRING ONIONS

Tasting notes: now this is some weird shit

xenophile
you're strange!
i'm strange!
we're all strange!
chew on that

OLIVE + CAVIAR THE WRONG WAY F

Tasting notes: thank you to susan; sometimes y
eat to realise you are hungry

a clear aspic on a mirrored surface distorts the diner's
reflection
enough to be unrecognisable
each gliding gel-taste of caviar(?)
each popsphere mouthfeel of olive(?)
i stare starry
the plate shimmers (star-touched) back
i don't know how much i don't know but i know that i will never
be this beautiful as looking down at what i cannot understand

?

RICE PAPER FLOWERS WITH RASPBERRY CENTRES

Tasting notes: rice paper does too have a taste because sight and smell contribute to our perceptions of flavour so there

IKEA has made
even
ROSES
ubiquitous and plastic

goddammit IKEA

what is even the point

when my best romantic gesture is so formulaic as to require
assembly instructions

GIN MERINGUE

Tasting notes: distilled   airy   dissolves on the tongue

st andrews
at christmastime
is so empty that it is full of ghosts everywhere out of the
    corner of my eye
tapping lightly on my shoulder massaging my temples
tugging my hood back pulling at a shoelace i run home
over ancient cobblestones
and hear their voices
try to confront this
icy vacancy

DINNER SERVICE

BREAD PLATE

Tasting notes: why don't more restaurants serve onion bagels? why is it always focaccia?

bitter onion clag mouth
molars glued back south
yawning yawing kith/kin out
i'm back in golders green

tube map last stop
crumbed fabric dropped top
caution! wet floor mop
i'm back in golders green

cold bones white stones
tea set milk groans
gran sitting stiff alone
i'm back in golders green

seeds burn bleach turns
nostril flare sharp gurns
gently lined up little urns
i'm back in golders green

is this my future not changing my own pants not cleaning
my own teeth hating johnny at the corner shop hating
silence noise the start the stop hoarse voice coarse spit
alone

i'll sit

stale   baleful

BUTTER KNIFE

Tasting notes: have you ever cut yourself with a butter knife?

we communicate through consumption
pressing artfully-cut black jackets into your arms like
slipping sweeties in the mouth of a crotchety belly-rounded child
downturned mouth honey-slow placated

mellified by shoes or issey miyake
when i have pressed butter-scrambled egg into my little sister's
mouth with my fingers and begged her to eat something
before you came home
before the *let's just go out*
mind if i stop in at westfield
you can get an ice cream when we were already so fucking
cold

i am brought on your shopping trips to russell & bromley for
the ninth pair of ankle-cut leather black boots with a sensible
        but flirty heel
a manufactured edge that will go unworn
there hasn't yet been a moment of realisation even though
you are vegetarian but you know i wait in hope
the one on oxford street may have different stock to the one
on regent street to the one in to the one in
i try on nothing
you don't offer a cursory *that would look good on you*
today's not a good trip
you've complained my clarks look shabby
i've just worked two sixty-hour weeks in them waitressing
for golfers looking for a different hole
they   my shoes   and i have started to go grey

the butter-soft black boots are spread out concentrically from
your thin-lipped gaze   a buffet of the same twenty times over
i watch you buy a week's wages worth of BLACK BOOTS and i
want to leather you for a brief vicious moment

that subsides to weary relief that we haven't argued yet
you didn't drag my sister and her 'massive feet' along
that the sharp   tongue has been sated
your elbows as pointed as your nails as pointed as the toes of
    the boots
and i have chinks in my carapace when i am so meat-soft
    underneath it!
and so hungry!

OYSTER FORK

*Tasting notes: eating an oyster is like stabbing a slippery alien
with too-human teeth – and getting away with it for now*

i am sitting at the station on the lethe line
cold toes aching knuckles counting time
by the horrific revolutions of a shadow down the carriage
it's a girl
it's a man
it's got a bone skull corvid head
and it spins
silent

the carriage is midnight void within
the station grows darker yet without
the shadow clings and spins on the strap hanging from the
ceiling
the adverts slip and change
the *evening standard*'s reeling from the final news
the seats buckle in on those who try for comfort and the
plastic metal arms fold and hold tight across the gut
the train is empty
but
the shape is dark against the white patterned deco tile
the shape turns
the shape smiles
next stop

SALAD OR FRUIT FORK

Tasting notes: surprisingly fruity   *surprising salad days*
insubstantial course

now is the winter of our disco tent
we're in a disco tent in austria
and they've remixed 'i will survive'
so now it's even g a y e r and
i've found my people – a martini
and a snowball – people naked top
up but swathed in ski gear at
bottom as if in the race down
the mountain to get to happy hour
they got too happy and decided an hour
was   too   damn   short

FISH FORK

Tasting notes: 'lachrymae' was once a really popular tune

grandmummy and granddaddy had an immaculate table
of inlaid wood with george killing a dragon
in the same way he plunged in the sword i aged twelve
took up a knife and attacked the piece of plaice

around us hung prints of shipwrecks and oil-painted canals
from their little venice flat with the bellboy and the grated lift
in surrey bungalow grandmummy looked up from her chair
wheeled to the end of the table
body slumped at a jaunty angle like a sail let down in calm
waters
perfectly curled hair clip-on pearls feet stuffed into too
small shoes bent inwards towards the stirrups arm
propping up her fork as it swayed towards her painted
prow
dainty
i clang down the fish fork
she inclines her fluted glass – cut crystal
sneaks furtive glance at granddaddy

granddaddy can grandmummy have some champers pleeeeeaase

she tells stories when well-oiled

    alright
he yells from the kitchen
spooning haricots verts into a shallow dish

thinning stooping knight in shining armour
lifting pushing slicing turning hauling writing
when she can't – he works
he remains in the kitchen while she entertains times long gone

tennis and the united nations
fast cars and waltzing

paris and everywhere
the six fluent languages and the further twenty in *thank you*
    and *hello*

i love them

MEAT FORK

Tasting notes: did you know fork *sounds like* fuck*? if you're very bad at saying the word* fuck*?*

meat wand
he inserted his love tool
it was throbbing   and dripping   and weeping
(because dicks... have tear ducts)
they frenched
even though they were doing it 69-style
it was hot
fuck
he said
fuck
fuck
ohhhhh god
he couldn't say anything except fuck
it was a condition
of the romantic persuasion
one of them put a hand around the other's neck
don't worry
permission had been given retroactively by kink checklist
inspired by *fifty shades*
sexy   sexy checklists
this is still while they are sixty-nining by the way
and one of them has a height difference
it was the culmination of their entire lives
the dick started to swell inside??? because
he managed to just get harder
because of the tight
heat
after insertion
fuck it was hot
their body was so warm
one of them clearly expected ice-cold orifices
it was like a fistula
squeezing around the cockstand
oh

oh fuck
fuck
the lube
was warming too
and tingling
they'd made it in a hurry before the passion got the better of
them
it was made out of melted sugar
which melts at 160 degrees celsius
because he wanted it to be hot and sweet
because this sex was a proof of their sweet love
they changed positions
they changed positions
they changed positions
they went back to the first one
their mighty swords of eros battled for dominance
at the same time as their tongues
it was a loving war
it increased in fever and pitch
when finally
at last
in conclusion
in summation
one of them mewed his pleasure to the stars
and
the great silky spearhead of his desire
thrust
thrust
and was no more

SERVICE PLATE

Tasting notes: in the plating style of so many new restaurants a solitary sad slab of concrete is all that remains of a service plate

according to insurance claims
natural disasters come in three kinds:
disease
man
and 'acts of god'

disease

i went to school during the outbreak of sars in hong kong
an outpost of a diseased empire
with white people like the walking dead
carrying out their old routines
quarantining themselves from an uncertain future
my first crush
(ng man him)
died age seven when sars reached the local population
i met more than four white people in one room at the
doctor's office
and we all wore face masks and cornflower-blue gloves for
six months
i'm still not sure whether this was
disease – because he'd caught sars
or man – because they didn't listen to a stoic boy when he
    coughed
or act of god – because white people always believe they
are saved by some higher power and not by the expensive
purell hand sanitiser

man

samantha
richer than kirsten of the oil and the museum and the $5,000
    halloween party

samantha
was abducted in a black mercedes
samantha was an american girl doll
pristine american dreams and fears
in my bedroom aged thirteen i played school (shootings/
    dramas) with samantha
they (black-clad barbies) wrote to her mother
her mother (raggedy ann) paid the ransom
she (a doll) came home with a haircut (safety scissors)!
i played her a natural disaster – natural
because samantha was rich and it is natural to target the rich
and it is natural to target girl children
at real school we had a lockdown drill
where you close the doors and pull down the blinds
and huddle in the school gym not moving
i'm still not sure whether this was
disease – it is an unhealthy mind that makes a doll individually
    traced blue tissue paper tears
or man – couldn't be
men were chronically free from my make-believe
or act of god – as i was god
no one should be that rich
and that lucky

act of god

in san francisco earthquakes sounded like gunshots
at least at first
people got blasé about both
let them blast let them blow themselves to smithereens
we'll smith bendy buildings to withstand the constant assault
we were taught an earthquake drill: find a shelter of a doorway
or under a desk
and cover your neck

we had a drug-dealing homeless guy who slept in the
panhandle park across the road

i knew his name to be larry cos he pissed on the side of
our building and the neighbours threatened to *shoot you
larry*

my figurine of a fairy fell off a desk – a category 6.0
and i dashed under my mum's doorframe
larry didn't have a door
larry went under a dying tree
and 'that bum' died with it

i don't know whether it was
disease – the tree was diseased and so was larry's love for
        bright postage stamps
i don't know whether it was
man – there are no shelter spaces left in so many beds in the
        city of space-age tech
no doorways to let him shelter
i don't know whether it was
an act of god
because in san francisco gunshots and earthquakes are
        unpreventable

because they are one nation under god

CARVING KNIFE

Tasting notes: salty and complex with a hint of pepper

did you know **chicken run** was adapted in slavic sequels?

chekhov's chickens:
chicken stop   chicken amble
chicken gallop – a poll apart
from the original   it was live
action and filmed in kiev –
the scenes were strongly flavoured
but predictable – and at the end
the chicken would attempt to flee
and fail and be eaten in front of a sunset

there was a greek chorus
– skewering the plot through the centre –
and when the inevitable audience
backlash raised itself from the groundswell
of discontent   the writers pointed out that
tragedy was foretold from conception –
the egg becomes chicken
ova and ova   and the chicken
tries for flight   fails   falls   and is fed on

the audience quailed:
fuck off anton   let the chicken live! if only on celluloid!

he clucked back:
the chicken lives in monologues   in half-spoken lies
in the pinkish livers   the chicken lives in the telling
in the clucking disapproval
and in the rapturous second   it takes to the sky

~~anton took a bite   licked his fingers:~~
~~the chicken lives in me   too~~

MEAT KNIFE

Tasting notes: unnecessary when in the right company

step 1: put on sue perkins and giles coren's *supersizers go*
bonus points if it's the restoration episode fall in love
with her again fight over who would win her hand you
or your friend

step 2: pour one small glass of wine pour one large glass of
wine

step 3: preheat oven to gas mark 6

step 4: buy a chicken

step 5: remember the oven is still on + rush through tesco

step 6: forget to buy tinfoil

step 7: prepare the chicken with some salt + pepper + olive oil

step 8: put chicken in the oven

step 9: confide light dislikes of mutual acquaintances

step 10: put on strange animation and quote along

step 11: check if the chicken is done (it isn't)

step 12: confide sexual secrets

step 13: *everyone should know how to confit an egg yolk*

step 14: refill glasses

step 15: check if the chicken is done (it isn't)

step 16: gordon ramsay cannot locate the lamb sauce

step 17: check if the chicken is done (it isn't)

step 18: push the one sharp knife you have into the breast
and thigh of the bird the juices should flow clear
like saliva like tears like purity of thought at this all
too infrequent meeting of fingers and women and
philia and pragmatic pragma pull the tray partway
from the oven abandon the knife tear straight in with
fingers there are talons at our extremities and we are
deadly the skin is delicious and fat feeds the most
gutpunching part of us the flat fades away and all that
is is only hunger and satiety women and chicken fire
and steel teeth and tongue civilisation is perfect and
more perfect is savagery and

the bones are picked clean in under fifteen minutes

FISH KNIFE

*Tasting notes: a fish knife should do no real work but part
the fish easy as moses parted the sea*

hunger parts easy as unwashed hair –
courteously impermanent – a state changed by a light touch
(meal deal   hair brush)
though despite a new centre parting or a satiety
the body remembers   and reverts to the old state of affairs

once a body has drunk neglect or hatred   or indifference
there is no immunity to the internal tendency to emptiness
tousling
and though you may be on a private path going towards your
        own lakeside villa
your mind remains staring into other depths   and says:
i should be on the lake   luck has filled me
i am still hungry   and need to brush my hair

SALAD OR FRUIT KNIFE

Tasting notes: a bruised pink lady apple flies through the air and lands on your plate

there's a pink lady apple-cheeked in flight

there are two shadowed men

they're green

my waist was grabbed
and pushed and and
and grabbed and pushed
and pushed and pushed
a shoe flies off

i pink
it's drink
their stink
arms swing
i trip

there's no ground
no grounding
the sounding
of the laugh
low too slow
too 'bro' to
keep a foot
on the floor
pastel mores
teeth tight but
enamel
white light on
my face/face
their bared teeth
cloaked   feral
joy mid-push

and i swing
suspended
the slick stem
knot ended
but wrapped
round fingers
swing seat loose
unstable
the swing
the table
i can't run
with no shoe
smile mid-air

catch breath catch self
so they don't catch
me they're two they're
too much in dark
shadows blurring
their features each
lurk with intent
i'm tense i smile

swing eyes winged winded
i wait that table

she's always going
to be in limbo

SOUP SPOON

Tasting notes: cereal is totally a soup and so is a milkshake
cos china has dessert soups so don't @ me you eurocentrist

linguistic arguments sound across the table
in a dive of an edinburgh flat in august
everything is bedraggled and thin   from the laundry
hanging damp over backs of chairs to the whole sixteen people
crammed in one room living cheek to arsecheek
we eat cereal at all hours snatched in rain gobbled in sleet
gnawn on when stale in small hours and we drink
mostly beer sometimes gin and we thin with walking
handing out hope after hope and begging to be seen
half-price hut to cut-price supermarket to cutting queues
whispering *i would never ordinarily do this but i have*
just got to see susan calman or sh!t theatre sorry sorry
cobblestone catching heels tearing open scabs when cabs
splash the walking dead hungry on their feet in clumps

i broke the bank at a ramen place
warm and quiet with wooden ladles in place of soup spoons
and thought of cereal

DESSERT SPOON

Tasting notes: 'nice with butter' is a bit extraneous on recipes as butter is basically lube for food you ordinarily wouldn't like

my stepmum stockpiles french butter in the second fridge
and shows off her haul of twenty sticks like instagramodels
with their bikini + gun selfies and leathery pouts
look at the spoils of war
let's make pastry with it
scarcity is d e l i c i o u s

(i hear it's nice with butter)

DESSERT FORK

*Tasting notes: the daintiest ending i can think of; please
take home and enjoy if you are filled up*

i ate a plum bakewell cake alone
the plums themselves sugar-crystallised tart
popping gently on the alveolar ridge   and
below sweet sand coating the tongue

my mouth was fully filled   and with each bite
there was: sun   soft leg hair   ice shards
grey smoosh-faced dogs   felt-tip pens

the suspension of each string of saliva
prolonged the facts of almonds   days off
bralessness   extremely large bees   peace

a swallow swooped by as i sat   and i watched
as it went up   up   and was obscured by light

i licked my fingers   stood from a stranger's stoop
and kicked pebbles carefully walking home

TEASPOON

Tasting notes: you can never go home again

it's 11pm we've eaten a bad mongolian meal and a good ice-cream meal i'm back in hong kong and speaking the language of my childhood after so many years i run my teeth over my molars taste houjichaa mochi softserve and i'm in the car he kept because i cried when he tried to swap it for a newer model that we now call the drug dealer car the good car's license plate reads tard15 we zoooooom round/up the hill centrifugal forces throwing my side against the leather door and my nose against the glass there's still neon and lights and bilingual signs we pull up to the tea shop it's like i never never left kennedy town went too far away became too different to return and the tea uncle says your face is too oily i just laugh thank him he pulls down metal drums of leaves and leaves we rinse the cups and lids of white furled buds to drink taste drink taste he says white tea is good for the stomach and the oil i say it also means i sit and think he says we need more time we all need more time to think i buy a catty as i leave with leaves he calls don't forget to store it in the fridge

i'm back in london after a sixteen-hour flight via mumbai
i cradle the plastic bag of wild vegetation with ballpoint
instructions on the glad part
slot it between the meal deal and the value mozzarella
close the white door
sit on the tiled floor

and cry

NAPKIN

Tasting notes: here's a blank page

LIBATIONS

WATER GLASS

Tasting notes: drinking water has no proven effect on the condition of skin

eyes are made of vitreous and aqueous humours
they're the oldest water
this liquid is more than four fifths of the entire damn thing you
    use every day
but old eyes are
rounded exceeding their lids' capacities
unblinking dry
my skin might be smooth enough
features young
but no one chooses the old eyes
off the cold meat display
the greying stare
it scares them

scares me too
i sit in the bath having chewed a lip bloody
cold iron tasting like 2013's sharp wrought railing
wondering what it's like to have a sense of humour
one that isn't stolen
from the loneliest bits of the internet
blue screen of death to squarer eyes

reaching for groundwater plumbing wells for uncontaminated
    sources
as if a blink doesn't refresh fully doesn't power cycle
reboot renew i know all water is recycled but just once i
would like to bathe myself   clean

CHAMPAGNE GLASS

Tasting notes: bubbly   fruity   very acidic

this yogurt isn't yogurt it's low-fat all-organic from the
only goat in nepal still giving milk   (pleb)
i bet you can't find it in shops

and my broccoli?
it's broccoli rabe actually
so bitter because i need everything bitter like
my unsweetened blue bottle cold roast cold brew cold drip
coffee
with rice milk because i'm lactose
intolerant

i've been buying only sri lankan woven fabric for my
cushion covers
organic
who cares how much the organic people behind the fabric make
i've diyed my whole house in batik
i saw it on goop and if gwynnie can crash diet a whole
country down to bird bones then so can i

i eat my desert before my dinner
quinoa tastes and looks like sand
tan granules that never end
my slate slab plate stretches for a metre

there's one chair at my table
wooden
no cushion
made from the last tree from that amazing african stock photo?
i think it featured in the *lion king*
this healthy healthy quinoa is
dry as the fields where some 'poor person'
has given me their whole yearly crop

how nice! how
sexy…

ooh this champagne? oh darling
how kind of you to notice! it is
organic
bio-wine
it's made from piss
that's why it's that colour
very healthy for you   just goes right through
i think it's made from hungarian orphan children's wee-wee
hahaha only joking

it's mine

we must recycle more
i've taken over the council's allotment with my compost pile
maria looks after it for me
don't you maria?
bring more champagne maria
MARIA
sorry you just can't get the help these days
MORE QUINOA MARIA

stuff those central americans i'm starving!
they'd make a fantastic centrepiece
organic
do come to my next dinner party? sexy fish is doing the
catering

bring nothing

it'll go so well with the hors d'oeuvres

WHITE WINE GLASS

*Tasting notes: the wine glass sweats in the right hands at
the right temperature*

tannins sweetly ring through us
in winter in front of the electric fire
stretching out time and legs

the hand
which once held a glass
is now empty – i fill it with your cheek
haptic pliant pleasing thing

sneaks on the floor
toes tipped in limbo
the shag pile to sink into
later

let's stay this unrealised
not move excepting fingerprints
a wine tart wanting

RED WINE GLASS

Tasting notes: some people who pretend to be vampires on the weekends have a very iron-heavy glass of red to keep them in the zone

bed death

this sexually transmitted virginity is making us vulnerable
to vampires

a man knee-walks up a bed to his négligée-clad wife

both smiles sharp

and forgets how to touch her

she rends the air   *was it sharon?*
screams serrated   *that slag*
he corrects her   *virgin*   *she had that*
sexually transmitted   virginity
touch me again for the first time   he pleads with a
bloody mouth
please   *i'm sorry*
she hurls the wrapped crucifix which   hung above their bed
out their iron-barred window
it slices her palm

her husband grabs for it gentle and bewildered
please   pulses through their conjoined flesh
he scared   she terrified and terrific
baring their teeth at each other in grotesque parodies of
smiles
quakingly and quietly   she reaches for the garlic
as he reaches for her breast

and he sinks forward   bloodless
neck snapped in the final submission

newfound virginity and innocence has remade him vulnerable
unsteeled by their shared history
he has crossed over the last line

he leaves behind dust in their bed

she threads her hands through silver sand

she pulls out a vibrator

BEER GLASS

Tasting notes: lambic sour   not for the faint of heart

here puss puss puss
sour puss puss puss
heeee-ya puss
pussy
mouth like a lemon butt but
less acidic than the response to that
tart-ass comment that some
limey bastard flung at her sour face *smile*
sugar tits and she smiled so hard

she cracked

her tooth and can only drink soup

the doc smiled snuck in *impressive did you report it*
she popping a cap carbonated rising to stand said *no*
now give me the drugs and let me go home

so she tiredly made soup for her van gogh lemon-yellow
head fermenting fury deep within her fizzing gut how
very dare he pulled down the soup pot splashing in a beer
stock she bashed in ginger gingerly moving her jaw and
wishing she could stuff a finger of the fiery root right in
his gob guess he'd like that   sick bastard   but
she couldn't give a fig for what he'd like – oh how he'd
burn removed the pot from flame she heads up to her attic

invites in a cool breeze
lets the nose of the city drift
across a muddled head

pours a beer
pops a pill
sips shallowly
opens herself to the air
rests   still   faintly tart   sour-pursed
and lets the soup pot settle

WHISKY TUMBLER

*Tasting notes: i'd invite you to close your eyes to better
suss out the flavours but this is a literary medium*

as a mariner himself

the deep slept beneath him
fires banked as he did
a bog stank round his craft
copper lined his eyes
a chewed strain of maize-fed him
the heat of the sky and the heat of the vents dark below –
he'd belch pot ale

as a mariner himself

he'd pour into spanish or american ports
whining low frothing violently
blending smoky bars with heavy spirit

as a mariner himself

the last feints on shore were brought back aboard
for the onward journey home

ESPRESSO CUP

*Tasting notes: caffeine queasiness should be expected
when nearly boiling water is forced through finely ground
beans at high pressure*

this job is only worth it for the free month-long railcard

everyone on the 7.43am tube has some obscure sadness
    pulling down their gaze
while above train tracks' buried route civilised london sleeps in
    early morning haze
a weary woman with foreign office lanyards leans against the
    glass partition
as the carriage rattles from overground into the gloom her
    glasses transition
a half-shaved businessman with black pinstriped suit and navy
    tie pushes out a sigh
his blankly staring eyes watch slow-ticking watch and the
    countless dark grey bricks rush by

i grasp the rail with fragile hands
too night-tired to truly stand
yet another journey in pinching heels
enjoy earning a mediocre £5 meal!
the jubilee line hums softly along
we sardined sway together in the throng
swiss cottage   st john's wood   baker   bond   green park
politician intern potential spy
disembark   lose each other by and by

as i grab a fortifying shot from the subsidised costa on the
    ground floor

i mutter: only got data entry for the conservatives one shite
    week more

TEAPOT

Tasting notes: oversteeped   sugared   body warm

home

had one

once hong kong egg tarts gluten heavy on my tongue gum
clagging on the inside of my teeth sweet
nothing fades to black background
dark grey ink city lights reflecting pink pollution solution
clean air green mango green jungle urban turban
cha maker yut bui lai cha mgoi soy
milk in everything because hipsters don't touch hk
'kay so i've got nothing on the brain but plenty in my kitchen
kitsch bento box kitsch smiling hello kitty chopsticks for kids
there's nothing in home that isn't

nostalgia

they're memory sense memory sense sensuality in every sip of tea
lai cha   chai   green   gunpowder   guns
colonisation a tangible warm arse-print on a whole 8 sq. km but
reassuring in the sense that someone has sat there before you
i've got no home but i've got tea and guilt and egg tarts
tart in every bite bit off words of the allegedly ugliest
        language fishwife
duk ley lo mo my lo mo is slow mo in my memories
there's nothing like the fabric rustle hustle bustle of
mum's skirt when she bends down and

time slows down molasses poured tea and she

kisses me on the forehead
why aren't you in bed –
tart words soft hands black skirts working woman develops
bitter across not just my tongue but my lungs breathing in
breathless deathless smog air heavy on my skin breathe in

i can taste the city in my every pore shoreline gritty looks
soft beaches not pretty covered in wrappers
wan chai is full of expat slappers everyone knows that goes back
every saturday night or tuesday every time is turn up turn up
place pale face free entry clubs for fourteen-year-olds who are
    still safe
the easiest city in the world to leave everyone does
eventually so no there's no home in hong kong people
can't last long

but in memory there's tea   and egg tarts
and me

COURSES

SOUP

Tasting notes: warming with the brightness of one small point of star anise

sat across from you in my dark cold flat
you talk about ska and sondheim
legs kicking off the stool and mine firmly planted

and i hug my bowl of soup tighter and tighter and
you look brighter and brighter and lighter and lighter and
    lighter and lighter…

you
the uptilted bowl held flat to my face by open palms

you're light
a truer star
the yielding yellow warmth like a bowl of chicken soup
with knödel
fat flecks on the top of golden broth
from the moment anyone sees you
like just the merest touch of your pupils can suffuse joy
across acres of cold skin
you soar warm across myriad constellations too far away
to burn but just close enough to nurture
you're just   right
kepler-22bravo   you're in everyone's
goldilocks zone
you dance fixedly while supporting the life around you

even my breath lifts and falls with the opening of your
eyelashes
look at the sun
the sum of your scraps and slivers and the strangers' lives
you touch is greater than the galaxies of thought i will
have to methodically unerringly specifically ploddingly
create

i tattoo a cinderblock on my table to warn people that i
cannot
will not
refuse to fly

there is value in being grounded

or so i hope

SALAD

*Tasting notes: freshly dressed with a ponzu vinaigrette
and millennial malaise*

i know i'm unwell when i watch *jiro dreams of sushi* and
my stomach does not register hunger

chewing is like wading through cement
the brownie i made when happier (which contains 85% cocoa
    solids)
is dusty and cloying
food has supplanted and been conflated with happiness in my
    brain – let me cook for you
let me eat with you
the unctuous delights of perfect cheese
the light decadence of uni butter angel hair pasta
the warmth and depth in a bowl of pho

all of these things i made for myself today
to try and break through the fog
but the cheese was just so much sensation
the uni an expensive failure
the pho just hot wet nothing

i look at these empty bowls on the lanolin countertop
the light dancing across the fat on my pho
the golden sensuality of the uni/butter compound
the yellow-white firmness of the globules of cheese where
light and my knife have touched it
and my stomach rumbles in protest
and my brain just goes
shh

jamie oliver
you've failed me
heston blumenthal
how could you
anthony bourdain
why?

i even retreat to alice waters
but salad is difficult to make well in scotland

and i now clutch on to the idea that if i only had the
perfect avocado
i could avoid depression again
bake an egg into it
sprinkle with sriracha or maybe thickened soy sauce or even
a rich red wine balsamic
fatty but light
rich but simple
the perfect smooth green unflecked by black strings unlike
the crap tesco counterpart
the perfect oval shape heavy at the base like a fertility idol
but i know this is a lie i'll tell myself
a light at the end of the tunnel

i   can't   wait   to   be   hungry   again

FISH

Tasting notes: everyone should gut a fish at least once

my eyes are two bruises
i still feel the cat hair inside my throat
when vocal folds rub like the gentle
touch of paw pads as i swallow sound
staring at the red plush seats next to
the red scratched suitcase
with the red blood dripping from a
cold-split lip and red nail-corners
peeled piles of off-cuts
and everyone is wearing headphones
and no one is listening to music
and there's one person coughing and
my throat itches inside   slide   saline behind stiff contacts
and it's oh so quiet the carriage as
we carry a last red spark to london
and in scotland everything was
purple purple purple
but the window shows that we on the
train are black   white   and red all over
i was read to sleep this afternoon and
woke to take the train and walked my
way into white noise and whined into
my cupped hands round my keep cup
keeping my head up because it's the
quiet carriage   and my carriage is
lumpen and back slumped
and with you everything was
purple purple purple
i don't want this to be a new year or a
new me or paint nudes on my lips or
hear nights of silence at red wood
restaurants
i want live wails of whisky and watts
of ugly-toothed grins and hard bar
stools and thistles

fucking
everywhere
because in scotland everything was
purple purple purple
because the long walk to the sea was
blue   and i am

well

re(a)d

MAIN COURSE

Tasting notes: remember that sirens sang to kill; that they were seductive was selective adaptation

entrez!
welcome in messieurs mesdames mesamies qui sont ni l'un
ni l'autre
eat

gorge yourself on the bread the butter already on the table
oh do help yourself to the salt flowering near the butter
dish – you are guest you are safe here – they welcome back
astronauts to earth with bread and salt you are clear to land

sip on water then champagne then cocktail then white
wine then red wine then cognac then coffee/tea – you are
hummingbird and deserve to flit through the garden – they
say everything in moderation especially moderation you are
welcome to be moderate another time

lean on the table your friends the waiter who comes to take
your order the old favourite dishes – this is a place of comfort
we love to have you here – they say that when the night is dark
you should lean on someone here we keep the lights dim for
you to choose that touch

eat! for all that is sacred eat! eat with friends enemies mere
acquaintances   dunk hands in dipping bowls or wipe on
tablecloths/ties between bites order one of everything
then another one of the favourite – this is where you can slot
food in for love love in for safety safety in for pleasure as you
sop up sauce with more bread – they say that to eat with
someone releases the same chemicals as staring deeply into a
puppy's eyes here we are warm soft we love you unswervingly

belch   chat   make conversation   fix the world and
despair about your place in it   expel the cares of outside for
now you are in the walls gulp cares like wine – this is ur-

connection after you see someone also yawn when you yawn
or catch hiccups of laughter or snot out of the nose when
booze goes down the wrong way – they say that to be in the
room where it happens is the best but be here   now   in the
room where nothing does

                                        pay your bill

                                                leave

                                        (come back)

entrez!
welcome in messieurs mesdames mesamies qui sont ni l'un
ni l'autre
eat...

PALATE CLEANSER

Tasting notes: a small sorbet of sweet meyer lemon and szechuan pepper

sometimes
i am lonely   enough to lie   on my side with my arm
trapped underneath my body[8]   letting it
go numb so that i can   pretend that someone else
is holding   me while i doze under the   cold
covers[9]
as i was told by society that[10]   i need   you to be there

sometimes
i am alone[11]   enough to wish that the static   silence

---

8   this is what we call harmful ideational language
                i've just dressed up self harm with some alliteration
        and internal rhymes in a three-part structure

9   i'm sorry does it piss you off that i've ruptured the spell of
        the evening
                created the illusion of depth
                romanticised death not skewered but punctured the
        patriarchy
                the poem deflating with a sad hisss

10   slam poetry is political
                it is accessible expressible affects the
        impressionable
                i can slam   i can share the hell i've been
        through god so long as it touches you

11   'help' a slam poem cries and sighs out the promise
                        welp
                        i'm not so sure   not anymore
                that this is the way to talk about rape
                how many metaphors does the bottom of the
                barrel have left to scrape?

around me would   blur into the fluffy pink
mist that happens when i stare at the setting sun too long[12]

sometimes
i press my fingers against my eyes lightly   and the
colours behind my lids go purple
then i press harder   and i can see that i   contain
entire galaxies[13]

pins and needles in my eyes   pins and needles in my arm[14]
either way it hurts to leave[15]   the cocoon i create for myself
in the comfort of my brain   and my blankets[16]

---

12   what is this worth?
                                another slammer ranting about their
          unfortunate relationship with birth with   love with
                              men with   depression
                  another predictable though true jam session

13   but one person's truth isn't enough not anymore
                                                                i'll call
          my own bluff

14   write a fucking sentence   that is not only true
                                          but important   to
          someone other than you

15   try   mate   just try to write something new

16   sometimes i hurt myself because i feel like i've been hurt
          enough already and i needed help
                                    thank fuck for therapists and
          that i'm not relying on spoken word as my only source of
          activism

HARD CHEESES

Tasting notes: what is a mouse without a cat? sincerity without expression?

i think we should get a cat
it would be fulfilling
for us
a warm thing that breathes and
it could
touch me
if it wanted to
i am more likely to get regular affection from
our cheshire-invisible cat than
you
my love
where were you
why are your legs fur-soft
damp to the touch
i left out an ignored sandwich
and it
rain-flecked
was there in the morning
whole
tracks of silence
stain conversation

i think we should get a cat
my love
a companion for greying
it too can scream from outside a window
forgets that doors once closed to a room open onto the same
view
the next time
brings home dead birds or packs of beer as a grisly trophy
unasked for
scorns cuddles on its own whims to its own schedule but when
    it wants
it wants
to be held

i think we should get a cat
my love
a radiator's purr cannot match a living thing in my bedroom
and a tap dripping in the house is not loud enough to cover
mine
my organic saline solution for a laptop mousepad

i think we should get a cat
my love
i'll name it constance

SOFT CHEESES

*Tasting notes: humboldt fog; in san francisco they named
the fog carl*

carl was blue   or was it grey   or was it gray –

hanging low on the hills bisecting the panhandle from the heights
from laurel-triumphant juice stores and heaving dim sum
clement weather winding through egg-tart-rich storefronts

carl sat heavy most days   soaked us lightly but we never
    wore jackets
just sturdy shoes and strategically torn muni passes and we
    walked up then down
yoga pants of puffed air misting large windows that craned to
    catch every sun particle
that carl couldn't block   we strode in flannel when carl
    knocked on our city's door

we talked about going out of the city   heading north or
    south or to tahoe
we'd camp queerly   each with a job:
you with the driving   you with starting the fires
and i was always assigned cheese   instead we'd walk to
    tj's or whole paycheck
and wear disguises for free samples   once we made it as
    far as point reyes
and used summer camp counselor money to raid cowgirl
    creamery for a taste of potential

*

carl sits pretty constantly between us
the cheese we chose had a layer of ash
undeniable alpiny goat-flavoured   stubborn
salt-etched   soft and crumbly
we discuss houses   mortgages   student loans
moves to germany or virginia

you've (not you the other you) stopped replying
        polysyllabically to change
'cool   sweet   nice'
words just don't cut it anymore   cheese-cutting jokes
stopped squeaking out giggles

carl was blue   or was it grey   or was it gray –
fog hanging low on our skype connection
it's here now   bisecting us from us
from the camping and the promises
from the city and invisible cities
from one half of fully fat-rich plans
and one half of ash

DESSERT

Tasting notes: sweet   *luxurious*   *far too rich*

this isn't just a love letter
this is an m&s love letter

dear mary berry
let me self-compote
don't tell me to choux
pastry myself to
your bulletproof bouffant
no soggy bottom
to that benthic-blue
depth in your eyes – i
just fall deep within
my well of affections smoother than gin
would you fancy a
tipple? a tickle?
of rosemary loaf?
that tangerine oaf
by your side – ditch him!
i'll gaily pitch in
just name your kitchen

oh mary-rosa
berry me among
your clouds of whipped cream
i'd taste your crème pât
that touch… vanilla?
saucy… but enough!
while custard's for birds
avian jackets
you wear loosely clasped
air encased when baked
and held like my gasp
lean over that bowl
turn easy-over
we'll eat those white-iced
hot cakes in clover

dear mary berry
each slick lick of lace
each piped hair in place
your marie rose-pink
confectioner's face
a tooth-rotting treat
for feasts at midnight
whisking up frenzy
into sweet stiff peaks
while oven-warm you
bubble and squeak – piqued
like my interest
taste your paris-brest
run away with me
to an ile flottante
for you – swear i'd be
no mere dilettante
i'd be yours for life
the compleat housewife

oh mary-rosa
bury me in bon
bons – that honey song
of sheer perfection
of truly scrumptious
don't they look tempting?
let's face it – i'm wooed!
i don't care how it's viewed!
i don't care if it's lewd!
(the prunes – they are stewed)
my fingers pruney
in your berry jam
my eyes gone moony
peeling 'part cured ham

dear mary berry
re: country secrets

i'm down to explore
rolling tidy tarts
you glide 'cross the floor
pre-prepped ballotines
will cater our wedding
a bit informal
(yeah you know where i'm heading)

dear mary berry
marry me
i'd feed your sourdough starter
i'd keep you stocked in gin
say yes – make me the
happiest woman
that there's ever been

no?

AFTER DINNER MINT

Tasting notes: the smallest thing that brings you joy

sunflowers dahlias baby's breath roses roses roses whole milk
2% milk 5% milk cream heavy whipping cream sour cream
chalk picture of a smiling cow eggnog eggnog eggnog bread
aisle sourdough sprouted multigrain bread pain au lait gluten-
free wholegrain sweet pull-apart aloha rolls cocoa almond
spread speculoos cookie butter caramel sauce chunky peanut
butter smooth peanut butter sunflower butter almond butter
tahini (tahini?!) ~~two-buck chuck~~ charles shaw wine charles shaw
wine charles shaw wine sierra nevada christmas beer sierra
nevada normal beer thank god the checkout line the hawaiian-
shirted saviours and the

SUGARFREE MINTS 'ALTOIDS' SMALLS
PEPPERMINT
WITH OTHER NATURAL FLAVORS
CURIOUSLY STRONG[17]

---

17   Proven to be sensorially stronger than grocery store
panic attacks, homesickness, bad breath, nausea,
vomiting, small talk, and sensory fogs of all kinds. Wake up.

THANKS

Thanks to all who ate with me.

Alternatively:

Cheers to the midnight facebook 'poem/pome/poyum?' people: Emily Hoyle, Miles Hurley, Hannah Ritchie, and Marc Kealhofer, thank you.

For encouraging the appetite/developing the palate: Ah Ba, Susan, Grandmummy, Granddaddy, the King family, Mummy, and Nishant Raj, thank you.

My poetry good fortune in a bad list poem:

1. First rights go right to Carly Brown and Michael Grieve for first daring me to speak and truthful rhymes to weave
2. Tristram Fane Saunders, who took me seriously when I was at uni ignoring my degree
3. Sophia Walker, for constantly pushing me to be honest about my mediocrity (couldn't ask for a more badass mentor, honestly)
4. FOR THE BOOMERANG GANG, YEAH, THAT BOOMERANG GANG,
     thanks for welcoming me to London with a bang
5. And what else can I say but thank you, Ms Phippard, cos you made me write silly poems about cheese and it was hella hard[18]

Nonsense and good sense were provided by the Discourse Tiem Crew: Lizzie Antell, Bekah Dyer, and Scott McDonald. Thank you for housing me and feeding me and drinking with me that bonkers New Year. Because of you i got half the gosh-darn book written, and then the other half. I love you.

---

18   None have made it into this book.

A BURP

After 'i lik the bred' by Sam Garland

Tasting notes: regurgitated but fond memories

my name is han
i haf thees frends
acros the werld
som werds i send
wile chattin meems
or all alone
becos of them –
i rote the pomes

Lightning Source UK Ltd.
Milton Keynes UK
UKHW041220030520
362587UK00004B/308